JAMAICA

Written by Sadie Hallworth

I0811458

COUNTRIES of the WORLD

PowerKiDS press

Published in 2025
by The Rosen Publishing Group, Inc.
2544 Clinton Street, Buffalo, NY 14224

© 2024 BookLife Publishing Ltd.

Written by: Sadie Hallworth
Edited by: Elise Carraway
Designed by: Miranda Tremere

Cataloging-in-Publication Data

Names: Hallworth, Sadie.
Title: Jamaica / Sadie Hallworth.
Description: Buffalo, NY : PowerKids Press, 2025. | Series: Countries of the world | Includes glossary and index.
Identifiers: ISBN 9781499449280 (pbk.) | ISBN 9781499449297 (library bound) | ISBN 9781499449303 (ebook)
Subjects: LCSH: Jamaica--Juvenile literature.
Classification: LCC F1868.2 H355 2025 | DDC 972.92--dc23

All rights reserved.

No part of this book may be reproduced in any form without permission in writing from the publisher, except by a reviewer.

Manufactured in the United States of America

CPSIA Compliance Information: Batch #CW25PK. For further information contact Rosen Publishing at 1-800-237-9932.

Find us on

Image Credits

All images are courtesy of Shutterstock.com, unless otherwise specified. With thanks to Getty Images, Thinkstock Photo and iStockphoto. Cover – DosanJones, Ashok Mehta, Andrey Panin, Anna Kosheleva, GoodStudio. 2 – KKulikov. 4–5 – Andrei Minsk, Vladimir Molnar, upslim. 6–7 – gmeland, KKulikov. 8–9 – Debbie Ann Powell, Zoran Karapancev. 10–11 – Rawpixel.com, Monkey Business Images. 12–13 – Danita Delimont. 14–15 – Words As Photos, Ievgenii Bakhvalov, artphotoclub. 16–17 – Monkey Business Images, Sabrina Bracher. 18–19 – StockphotoVideo, photoyh. 20–21 – from my point of view, Craig F Scott, Drizzyphotographyja. 22–23 – Lost Mountain Studio, Mercedes Lisón Martín, CC BY-SA 2.5 ES via Wikimedia Commons.

CONTENTS

Words that look like this can be found in the glossary on page 24.

WHERE IS JAMAICA?

Jamaica is an island in the Caribbean Sea. The capital city of Jamaica is Kingston.

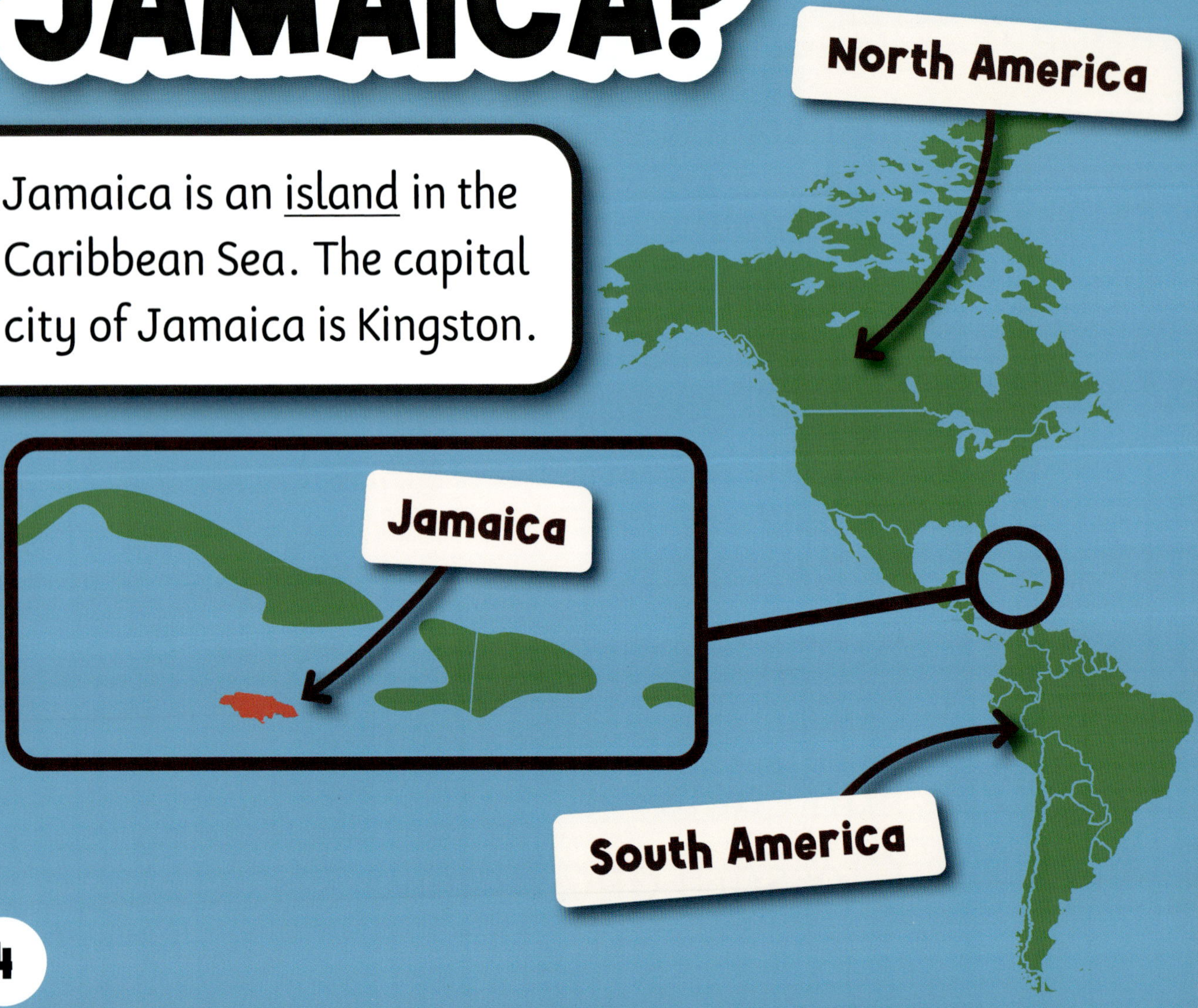

Jamaica's <u>official</u> language is English. Many people visit Jamaica for the hot weather and to spend time at the beach.

LANDSCAPE AND WEATHER

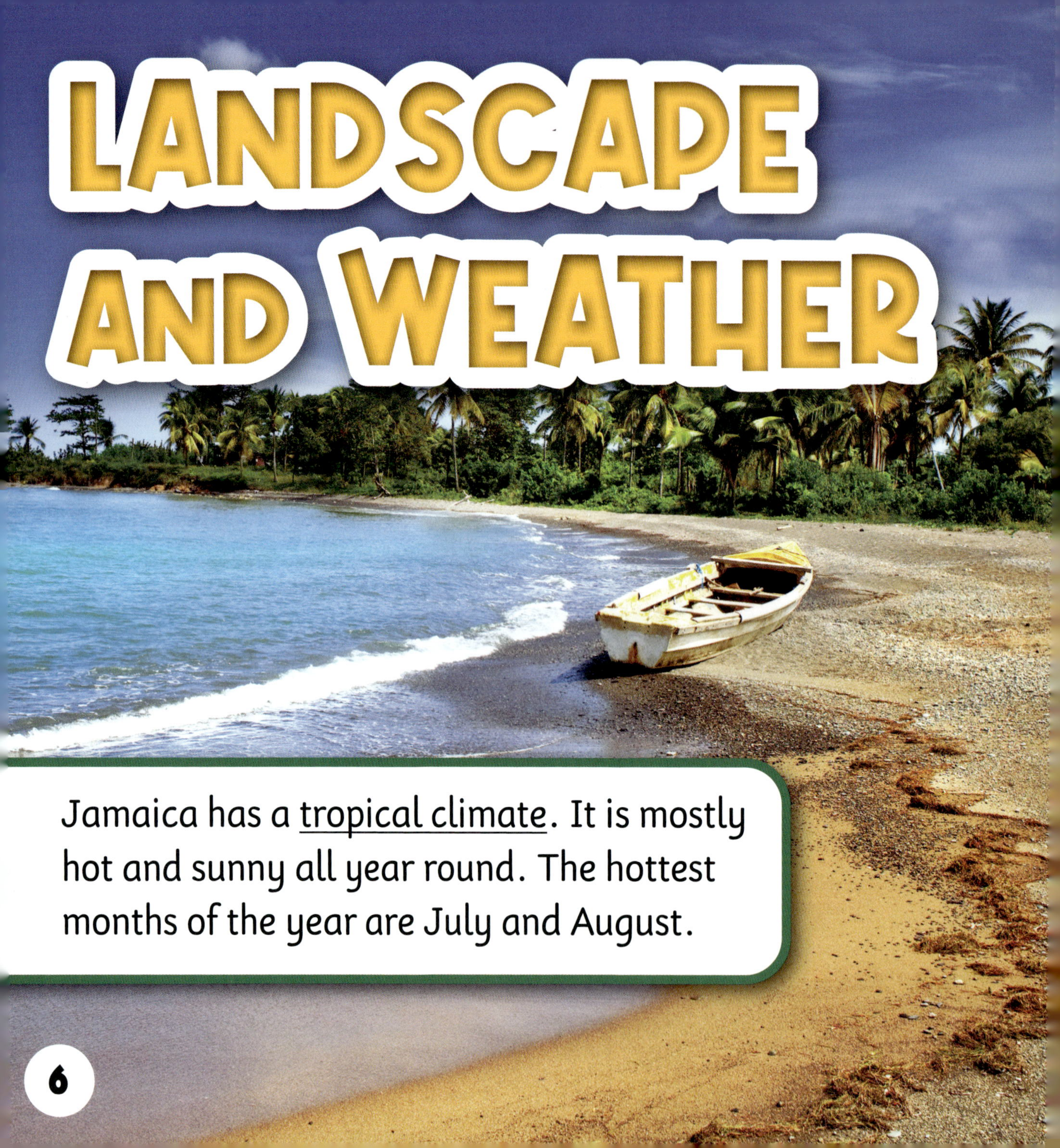

Jamaica has a tropical climate. It is mostly hot and sunny all year round. The hottest months of the year are July and August.

Jamaica has many tropical rainforests, high mountains, and flowing waterfalls. Dunn's River Falls is one of Jamaica's most famous waterfalls.

Dunn's River Falls, Jamaica

RELIGION

There are many religions in Jamaica. Jamaica's most followed religion is Christianity. A Christian place of worship is a church.

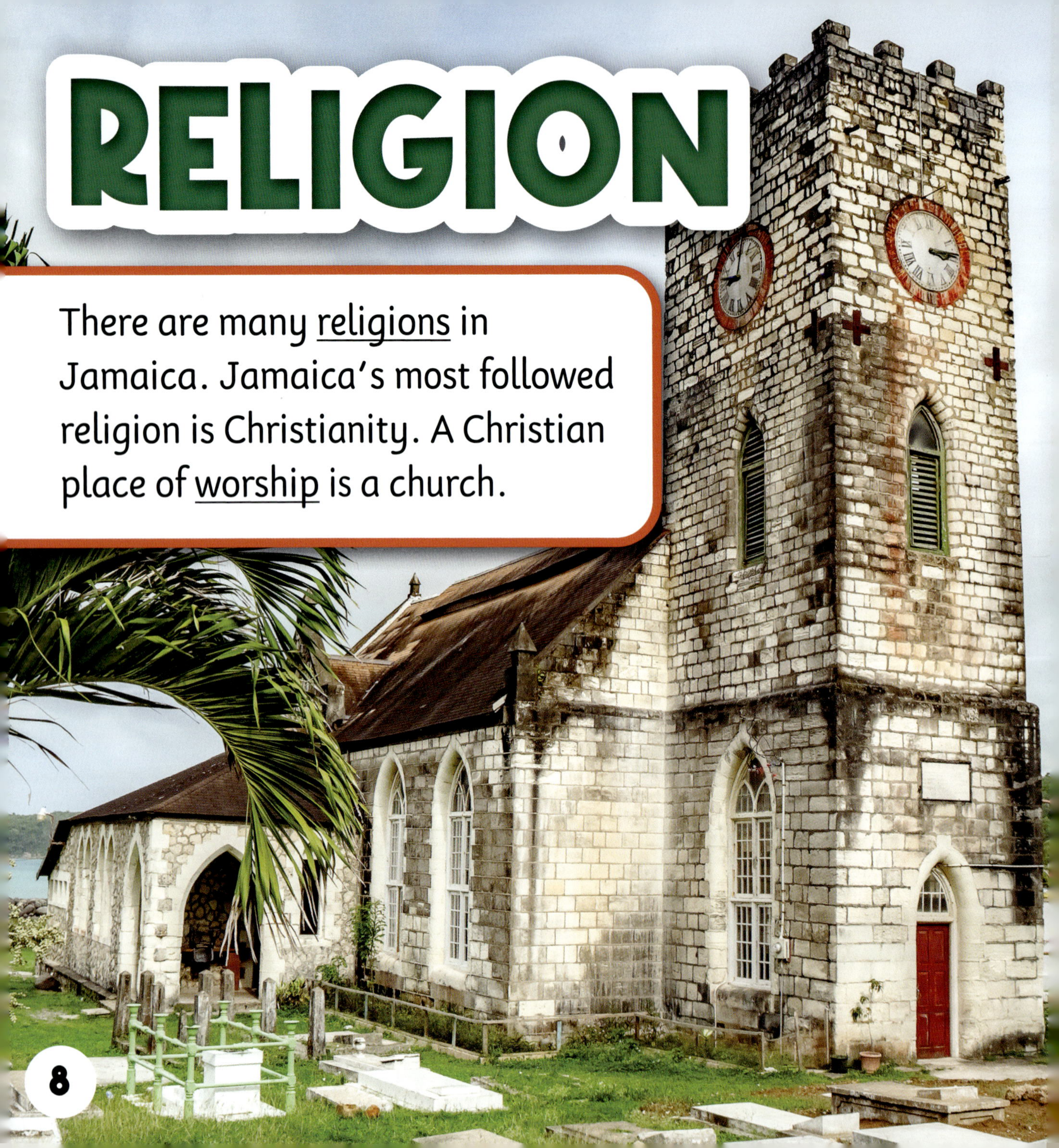

Many Christians go to church every Sunday for prayer. Christians also go to church to worship God and read from the Christian holy book, called the Bible.

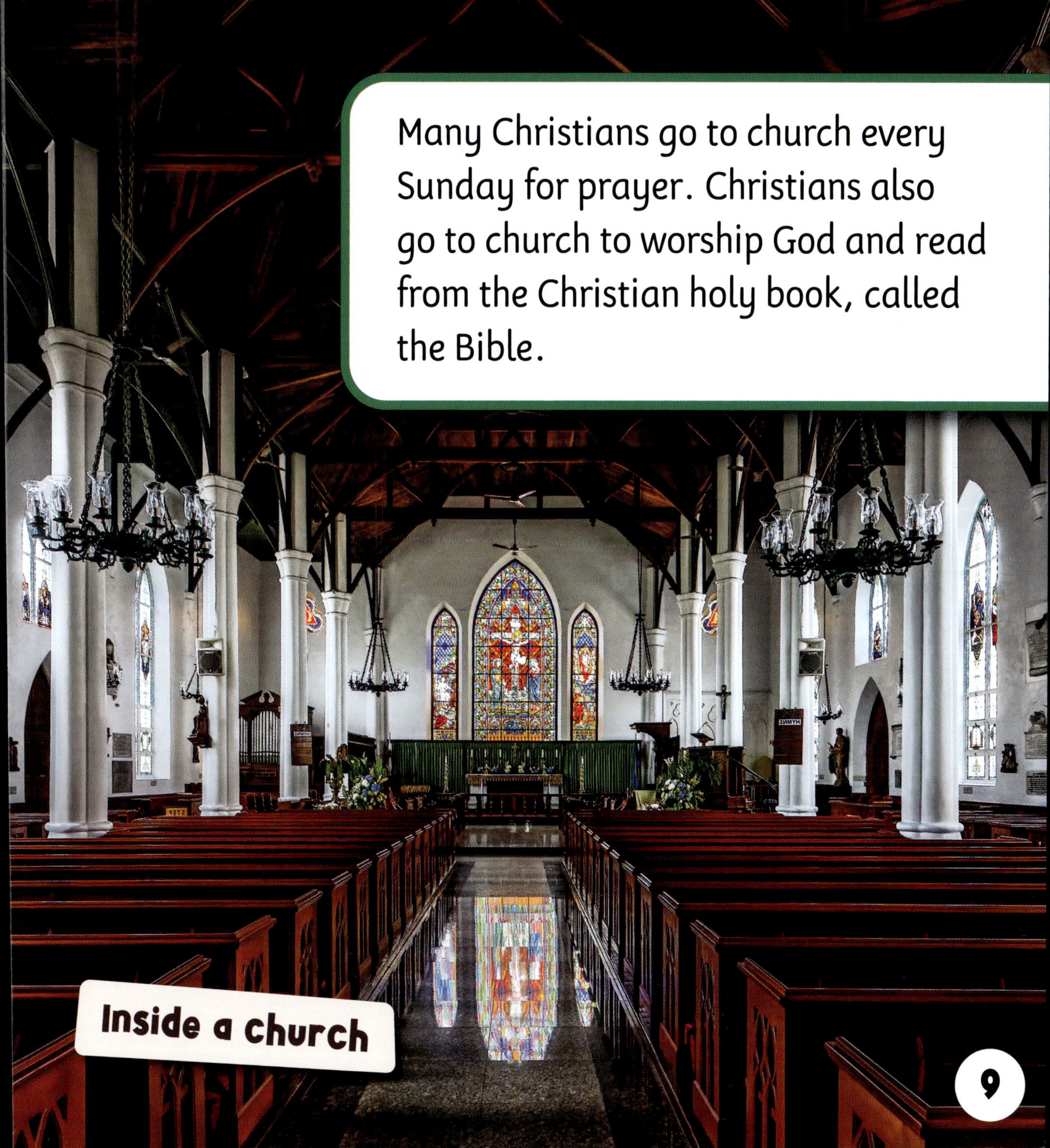

Inside a church

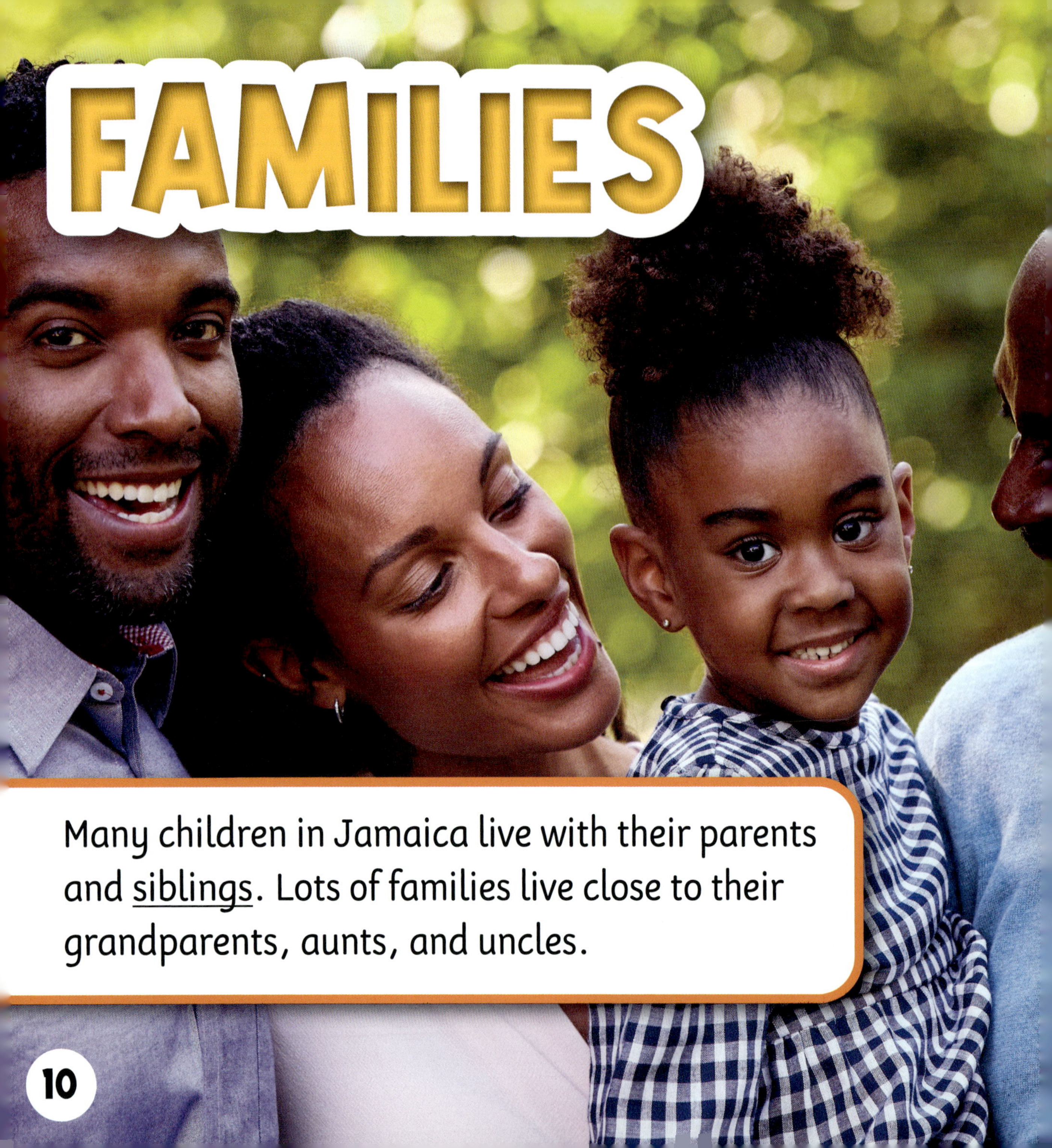

FAMILIES

Many children in Jamaica live with their parents and siblings. Lots of families live close to their grandparents, aunts, and uncles.

Families get together for special occasions such as birthdays and weddings.

SCHOOL

Children in Jamaica start school at the age of six. Most Jamaican schoolchildren wear a uniform.

At school, children learn English, math, and science. They also often learn how to play sports, such as soccer and cricket.

HOME

Most people in Jamaica live in big cities and towns, such as Kingston and Portmore.

Some people in Jamaica live in small villages or on farms. They often grow crops, such as coffee beans and sugarcane.

CLOTHING

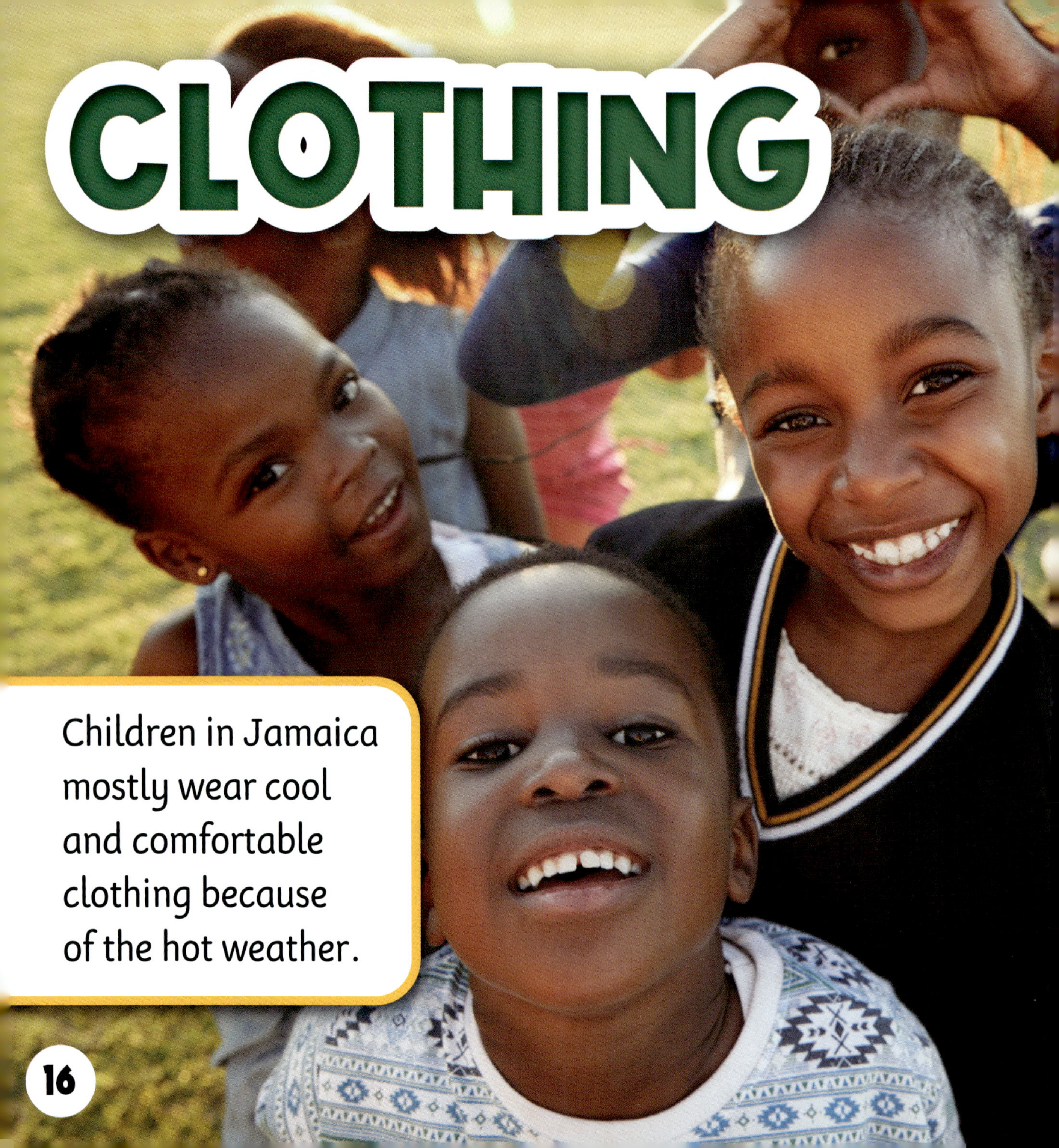

Children in Jamaica mostly wear cool and comfortable clothing because of the hot weather.

Many Jamaican women wear traditional headscarves. They are made out of soft, colorful cotton and are wrapped around the head.

SPORTS

One of the most popular sports in Jamaica is track and field. This includes running, jumping, and throwing.

The Jamaican athlete Usain Bolt is believed to be one of the fastest runners in the world. He has won many Olympic gold medals.

FOOD

Jerk is a traditional style of cooking in Jamaica. This is when meat is cooked with hot spices over a small fire.

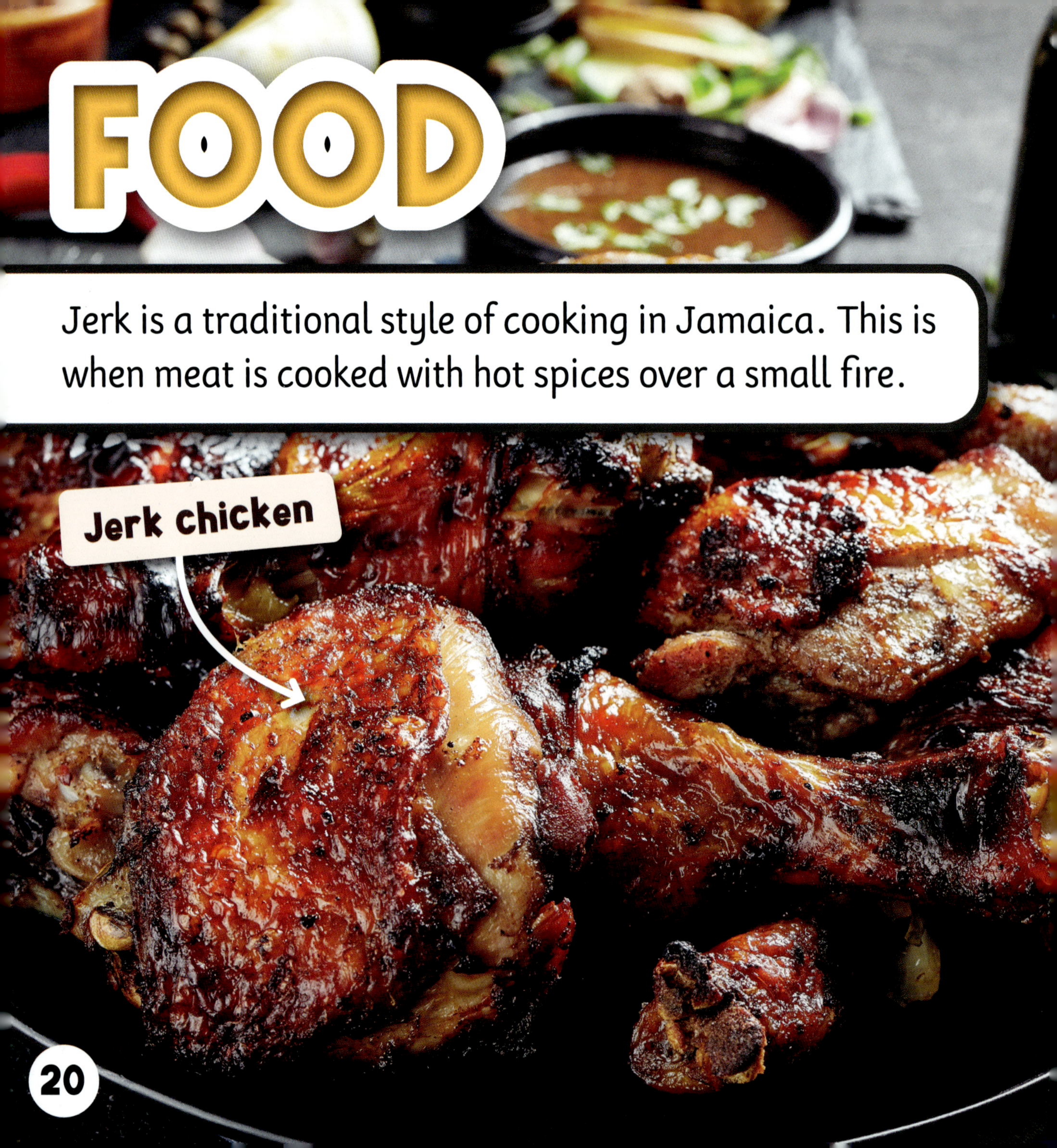

Ackee is the national fruit of Jamaica. It is often cooked with salty fish and served for breakfast.

FUN FACTS

Reggae music was created in Jamaica and has become a very popular type of music all around the world.

The giant swallowtail is the largest butterfly in Jamaica. Its wings can be 5.5 inches (14 cm) wide!

GLOSSARY

athlete someone who is skilled at sport

crops plants that are grown on a large scale to be eaten or used

island an area of land that is surrounded by water

national to do with things that are shared by people in a country

official to do with something that is recognized as having power or being important

religions systems of faith and worship, especially to do with a god or gods

siblings brothers and sisters

traditional to do with beliefs, customs, or ways of behaving that have been around for a long time

tropical climate warm and wet weather

worship religious acts of praise, such as prayer

INDEX